Paging Dr Freud Dream Journal
Published by Kinkajou
Copyright © Frances Lincoln Limited 2015

A catalogue record for this book is available from the British Library

Freud illustrations by Mark Mason. All other images courtesy of
Shutterstock and © Copyright individual copyright holders.
Design by www.smartdesignstudio.co.uk

Kinkajou is an imprint of Frances Lincoln Limited
74–77 White Lion Street
London N1 9PF
www.kinkajou.com

ISBN: 978-0-7112-3683-7

Printed in China

9 8 7 6 5 4 3 2 1

MIX
Paper from
responsible sources
FSC® C008047

# PAGING DR FREUD
## DREAM JOURNAL

'DREAMS ARE THE ROYAL
ROAD TO THE UNCONSCIOUS'
– SIGMUND FREUD

kinkajou

**SIGMUND FREUD (1856 - 1939)** was an Austrian neurologist who became known as the father of psychoanalysis. Using dialogue with his patients as a clinical treatment, he developed techniques such as free association to identify and cure their mental problems.

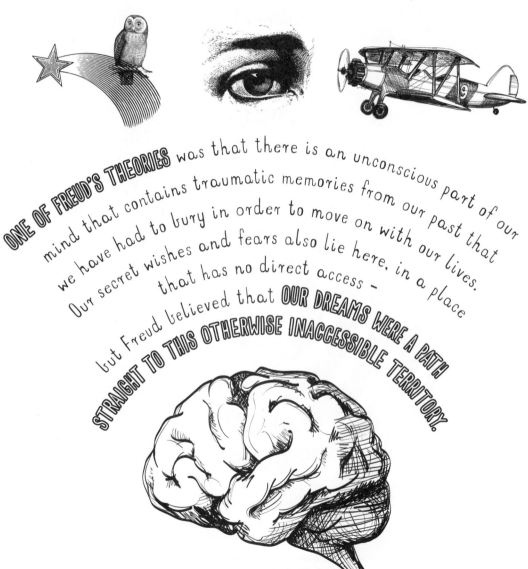

ONE OF FREUD'S THEORIES was that there is an unconscious part of our mind that contains traumatic memories from our past that we have had to bury in order to move on with our lives. Our secret wishes and fears also lie here, in a place that has no direct access – but Freud believed that OUR DREAMS WERE A PATH STRAIGHT TO THIS OTHERWISE INACCESSIBLE TERRITORY.

Freud believed that dreams could be understood on two levels: MANIFEST (REMEMBERED EXPERIENCES) and LATENT (HIDDEN MEANING).

## ID
is our unconscious, impulsive part which works to satisfy our primitive instincts and emotions.

## EGO
is the part of our mind that deals with our conscious awareness.

## SUPEREGO
handles our morality to ensure we are socially acceptable.

According to Freud, it is our EGO and SUPEREGO that guide our behaviour during the day, but when we sleep the ID takes over to battle our buried emotions and remembered experiences. It is our moralistic superego that causes us to forget most of our dreams when we wake up.

## FREUD'S FIVE CATEGORIES OF DREAM ANALYSIS:

DISPLACEMENT – the dreamer's own desire for one person or object is represented by a different person or object.

PROJECTION – the dreamer projects their desires onto another person.

SYMBOLISATION – the dreamer creates a metaphor to replace their unconscious desires.

CONDENSATION – the dreamer disguises their feelings and desires by reducing them to become an image or small event in a dream.

RATIONALISATION – the dreamer begins to wake and attempts to organise the parts of the dream that are puzzling to the conscious into something more logical.

Freud classed some dreams as being 'typical' and believed that there are universal symbols in dreams that can be used to interpret them. These symbols can be associated by shape, function, action or status with the things that we consciously find difficult to acknowledge. The symbols in your dreams may be typical, but can also have a personal meaning. Keep a record of symbols that appear in your dreams and note what they might mean to you.

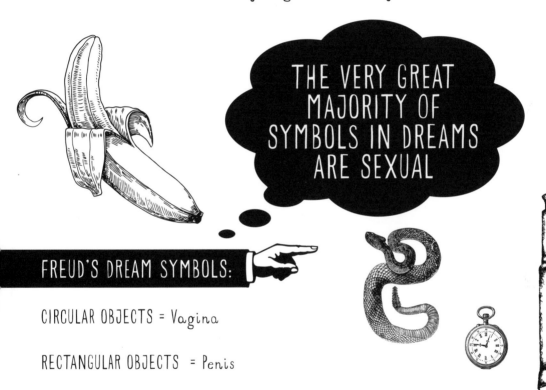

THE VERY GREAT MAJORITY OF SYMBOLS IN DREAMS ARE SEXUAL

FREUD'S DREAM SYMBOLS:

CIRCULAR OBJECTS = Vagina

RECTANGULAR OBJECTS = Penis

SEPARATION OF A PART FROM THE WHOLE SUCH AS LOSING A TOOTH = Castration

ACTIONS SUCH AS CLIMBING STAIRS OR DANCING = Coitus

WILD ANIMAL SUCH AS A LION = Passion

KING = Father          QUEEN = Mother

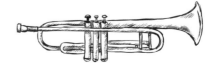

MY DREAM SYMBOLS:

Freud used the technique of **FREE ASSOCIATION** to interpret dreams. He first dissected the dreams of his patients and analysed them in parts rather than as a whole. He then asked his patient for the first thought that came into his or her mind on being told the analysis.

As everyone is different this is difficult to do: the same dream symbol may have different meanings depending on the individual.

THE **FIRST THING** THAT COMES INTO MY MIND:

MANIFEST ☐

LATENT ☐

NO IDEA! ☐

SYMBOLS HEREIN:

MANIFEST ☐

LATENT ☐

NO IDEA! ☐

SYMBOLS HEREIN:

My DREAMS are the royal road to my unconscious...

MANIFEST ☐

LATENT ☐

NO IDEA! ☐

SYMBOLS HEREIN:

SYMBOLS HEREIN:

My DREAMS are the royal road to my unconscious...

'Sometimes a cigar
is JUST a cigar.'

MANIFEST ☐

LATENT ☐

NO IDEA! ☐

SYMBOLS HEREIN:

MANIFEST ☐

LATENT ☐

NO IDEA! ☐

SYMBOLS HEREIN:

My DREAMS are the royal road to my unconscious...

MANIFEST ☐

LATENT ☐

NO IDEA! ☐

SYMBOLS HEREIN:

MANIFEST ☐

LATENT ☐

NO IDEA! ☐

## SYMBOLS HEREIN:

My DREAMS are the royal road to my unconscious...

MANIFEST ☐

LATENT ☐

NO IDEA! ☐

SYMBOLS HEREIN:

MANIFEST ☐

LATENT ☐

NO IDEA! ☐

SYMBOLS HEREIN:

'a child sucking at his mother's breast has become the prototype of every relation of love. The finding of an object is in fact a refinding of it; and, furthermore, introducing object loss as an unavoidable step in the path to mental evolution, that it is only later that the instinct loses that object, just at the time, perhaps, when the child is able to form a total idea of the person to whom the organ that is giving him satisfaction belongs.'

My DREAMS are the royal road to my unconscious...

MANIFEST ☐

LATENT ☐

NO IDEA! ☐

## SYMBOLS HEREIN:

My DREAMS are the royal road to my unconscious...

MANIFEST ☐

LATENT ☐

NO IDEA! ☐

SYMBOLS HEREIN:

My DREAMS are the royal road to my unconscious...

SYMBOLS HEREIN:

My DREAMS are the royal road to my unconscious...

SYMBOLS HEREIN:

SYMBOLS HEREIN:

'After all, we did not invent symbolism; it is a universal age-old activity of the human imagination.'

MANIFEST ☐

LATENT ☐

NO IDEA! ☐

SYMBOLS HEREIN:

My DREAMS are the royal road to my unconscious...

MANIFEST ☐

LATENT ☐

NO IDEA! ☐

## SYMBOLS HEREIN:

My DREAMS are the royal road to my unconscious...

MANIFEST ☐

LATENT ☐

NO IDEA! ☐

SYMBOLS HEREIN:

MANIFEST ☐

LATENT ☐

NO IDEA! ☐

SYMBOLS HEREIN:

My DREAMS are the royal road to my unconscious...

MANIFEST ☐

LATENT ☐

NO IDEA! ☐

SYMBOLS HEREIN:

My DREAMS are the royal road to my unconscious...

MANIFEST ☐

LATENT ☐

NO IDEA! ☐

SYMBOLS HEREIN:

My DREAMS are the royal road to my unconscious...

'Woman, whom culture has burdened with the heavier load
(especially in propagation) ought to be judged with tolerance
and forbearance in areas where she has lagged behind man.'

MANIFEST ☐

LATENT ☐

NO IDEA! ☐

**SYMBOLS HEREIN:**

MANIFEST ☐

LATENT ☐

NO IDEA! ☐

SYMBOLS HEREIN:

My DREAMS are the royal road to my unconscious...

MANIFEST ☐

LATENT ☐

NO IDEA! ☐

SYMBOLS HEREIN:

My DREAMS are the royal road to my unconscious...

MANIFEST

LATENT

NO IDEA!

SYMBOLS HEREIN:

My DREAMS are the royal road to my unconscious...

SYMBOLS HEREIN:

My DREAMS are the royal road to my unconscious...

MANIFEST ☐

LATENT ☐

NO IDEA! ☐

## SYMBOLS HEREIN:

'The business of analysis is to secure the best possible conditions for the functioning of the ego; when this has been done analysis has accomplished its task.'

MANIFEST ☐

LATENT ☐

NO IDEA! ☐

## SYMBOLS HEREIN:

SYMBOLS HEREIN:

MANIFEST ☐

LATENT ☐

NO IDEA! ☐

SYMBOLS HEREIN:

My DREAMS are the royal road to my unconscious...

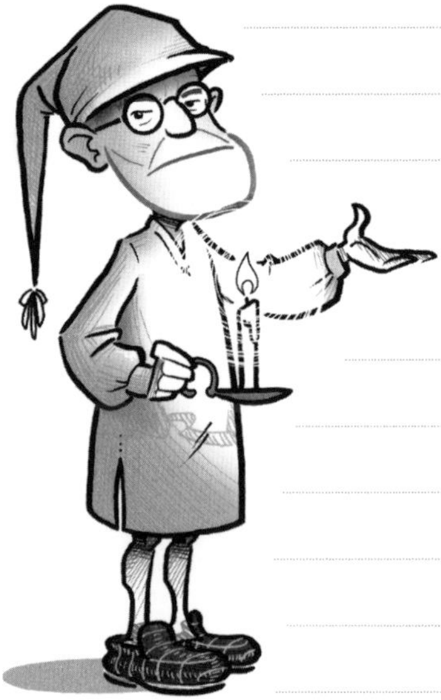

MANIFEST ☐

LATENT ☐

NO IDEA! ☐

SYMBOLS HEREIN:

My DREAMS are the royal road to my unconscious...

MANIFEST ☐

LATENT ☐

NO IDEA! ☐

SYMBOLS HEREIN:

My DREAMS are the royal road to my unconscious...

MANIFEST ☐

LATENT ☐

NO IDEA! ☐

SYMBOLS HEREIN:

My DREAMS are the royal road to my unconscious...

'THE FIRST HUMAN WHO HURLED AN INSULT INSTEAD OF A STONE WAS THE FOUNDER OF CIVILISATION.'

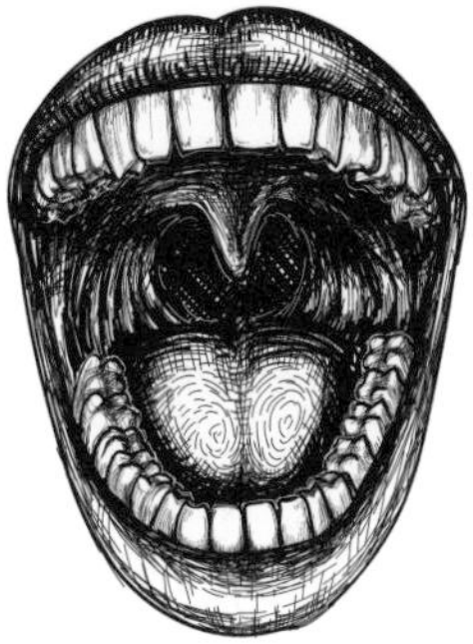

MANIFEST ☐

LATENT ☐

NO IDEA! ☐

SYMBOLS HEREIN:

My DREAMS are the royal road to my unconscious...

MANIFEST ☐

LATENT ☐

NO IDEA! ☐

SYMBOLS HEREIN:

My DREAMS are the royal road to my unconscious...

MANIFEST ☐

LATENT ☐

NO IDEA! ☐

## SYMBOLS HEREIN:

My DREAMS are the royal road to my unconscious...

MANIFEST ☐

LATENT ☐

NO IDEA! ☐

SYMBOLS HEREIN:

SYMBOLS HEREIN:

My DREAMS are the royal road to my unconscious...

MANIFEST ☐

LATENT ☐

NO IDEA! ☐

SYMBOLS HEREIN:

My DREAMS are the royal road to my unconscious...

'Being entirely
HONEST with oneself
is a good exercise.'

MANIFEST ☐

LATENT ☐

NO IDEA! ☐

SYMBOLS HEREIN:

My DREAMS are the royal road to my unconscious...

MANIFEST ☐

LATENT ☐

NO IDEA! ☐

SYMBOLS HEREIN:

MANIFEST ☐

LATENT ☐

NO IDEA! ☐

SYMBOLS HEREIN:

My DREAMS are the royal road to my unconscious...

SYMBOLS HEREIN:

'A man should not strive to eliminate his complexes,
but to get into accord with them; they are legitimately
what directs his conduct in the world.'

MANIFEST ☐

LATENT ☐

NO IDEA! ☐

SYMBOLS HEREIN:

My DREAMS are the royal road to my unconscious...

MANIFEST ☐

LATENT ☐

NO IDEA! ☐

SYMBOLS HEREIN:

'Every normal person, in fact, is only normal on the average.
His ego approximates to that of the psychotic in some part or
other and to a greater or lesser extent.'

SYMBOLS HEREIN:

My DREAMS are the royal road to my unconscious...

MANIFEST ☐

LATENT ☐

NO IDEA! ☐

SYMBOLS HEREIN:

My DREAMS are the royal road to my unconscious...

MANIFEST ☐

LATENT ☐

NO IDEA! ☐

SYMBOLS HEREIN:

My DREAMS are the royal road to my unconscious...

SYMBOLS HEREIN:

My DREAMS are the royal road to my unconscious...

'LOOK INTO THE DEPTHS OF YOUR OWN SOUL and learn first to know yourself, then you will understand why this illness was bound to come upon you and perhaps you will thenceforth avoid falling ill.'

MANIFEST ☐

LATENT ☐

NO IDEA! ☐

SYMBOLS HEREIN:

MANIFEST ☐

LATENT ☐

NO IDEA! ☐

## SYMBOLS HEREIN:

My DREAMS are the royal road to my unconscious...

MANIFEST ☐

LATENT ☐

NO IDEA! ☐

SYMBOLS HEREIN:

My DREAMS are the royal road to my unconscious...

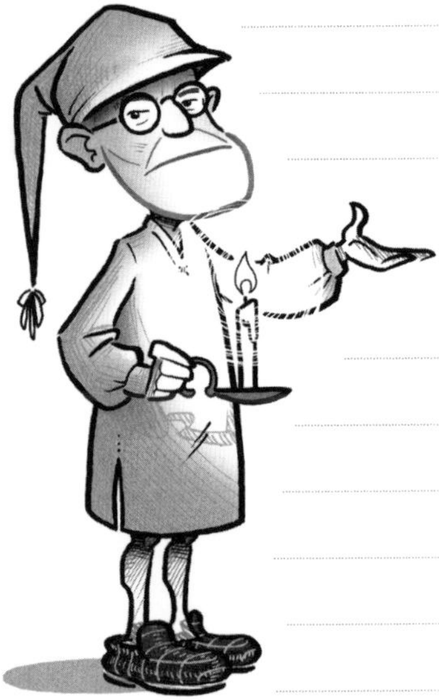

SYMBOLS HEREIN:

My DREAMS are the royal road to my unconscious...

'It is always possible to bind together a considerable number of people in love, so long as there are other people left over to receive the manifestations of their aggression.'

MANIFEST ☐

LATENT ☐

NO IDEA! ☐

SYMBOLS HEREIN:

My DREAMS are the royal road to my unconscious...

SYMBOLS HEREIN:

SYMBOLS HEREIN:

'Just as a cautious businessman avoids investing all his capital in one concern, so wisdom would probably admonish us also not to anticipate all our happiness from one quarter alone.'

MANIFEST ☐

LATENT ☐

NO IDEA! ☐

SYMBOLS HEREIN:

My DREAMS are the royal road to my unconscious...

MANIFEST ☐

LATENT ☐

NO IDEA! ☐

SYMBOLS HEREIN:

NOTES TO MY ID

NOTES
TO MY ID

NOTES TO MY EGO

NOTES TO MY EGO

NOTES TO MY EGO

NOTES TO MY EGO

NOTES TO MY EGO

# NOTES TO MY SUPEREGO

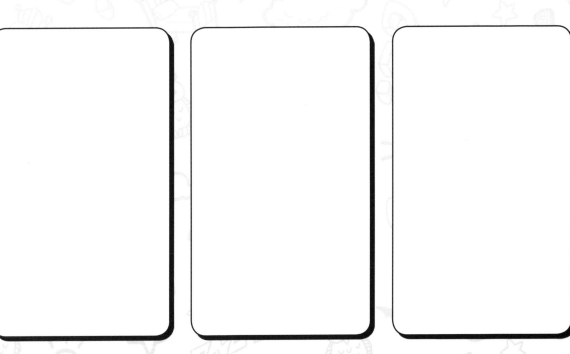

# NOTES TO MY SUPEREGO

# NOTES TO MY SUPEREGO

# NOTES TO MY SUPEREGO